PRINCEWILL LAGANG

Wise Courtship: A Christian Guide to Finding The One

First published by PRINCEWILL LAGANG 2023

Copyright © 2023 by Princewill Lagang

All rights reserved. No part of this publication may be reproduced, stored or transmitted in any form or by any means, electronic, mechanical, photocopying, recording, scanning, or otherwise without written permission from the publisher. It is illegal to copy this book, post it to a website, or distribute it by any other means without permission.

This novel is entirely a work of fiction. The names, characters and incidents portrayed in it are the work of the author's imagination. Any resemblance to actual persons, living or dead, events or localities is entirely coincidental.

Princewill Lagang asserts the moral right to be identified as the author of this work.

First edition

This book was professionally typeset on Reedsy.
Find out more at reedsy.com

Contents

1	The Quest for True Love	1
2	The Foundation of Faith	3
3	Preparing Your Heart and Mind	6
4	Navigating the Dating Landscape	9
5	Building a Deeper Connection	12
6	Discerning "The One"	15
7	The Journey of Commitment	18
8	A Lifelong Journey	22
9	Nurturing Love and Partnership	25
10	Weathering Life's Storms	29
11	Chapter 11	33
12	Celebrating a Lifetime of Love	37

1

The Quest for True Love

Title: "Wise Courtship: A Christian Guide to Finding The One"

In a small, peaceful town nestled amidst rolling hills and lush forests, a young woman named Emily found herself at a crossroads. Her heart ached with longing, not for fleeting romances or momentary infatuations, but for a deep and abiding love that would stand the test of time. She longed for a love rooted in faith, shared values, and a common journey towards God. As she gazed out of her bedroom window one evening, the sun setting in the horizon, she wondered if it was possible to find such a love in the modern world.

This is the story of Emily's journey, a journey guided by faith, wisdom, and a steadfast belief in the power of prayer. It's a journey she embarks upon in search of "The One" — the person God has ordained for her, a partner with whom she can share her life, values, and dreams.

As Christians, we often hear the phrase "God has a plan" and "His timing is perfect." But what does that really mean when it comes to finding a life partner? How can we actively seek out God's guidance while navigating the challenges of dating, relationships, and courtship in the 21st century? This guide, "Wise Courtship: A Christian Guide to Finding The One," is designed to help you answer these questions and more.

The desire to find a life partner who shares our Christian faith and values is a quest that resonates with many. Emily's journey, while unique to her, serves as an archetype for anyone who seeks to navigate the complexities of modern romance with a steadfast commitment to their faith.

In this first chapter, we'll explore the foundational principles of wise courtship and the significance of faith in the process. We'll delve into the idea that love is a divine gift and that God has a unique plan for each of us when it comes to matters of the heart. We'll also discuss the importance of self-discovery and readiness before embarking on this quest.

Emily, like you, is on a journey of faith, trust, and perseverance, as she waits upon the Lord's perfect timing. Her quest is a testament to the power of prayer, the strength of self-discovery, and the unwavering belief that God will guide her towards "The One."

So, as we begin this journey with Emily, let us first open our hearts and minds to the possibility of God's perfect plan for our love lives. Love, after all, is a divine gift that deserves our careful attention and our faithful pursuit. In the chapters that follow, we'll delve deeper into the practical aspects of wise courtship and the steps Emily takes towards finding "The One." But for now, let us embark on this voyage with open hearts and minds, ready to explore the depths of faith, love, and the eternal quest for true, God-ordained love.

2

The Foundation of Faith

Title: "Wise Courtship: A Christian Guide to Finding The One"

Emily knew that her journey towards finding "The One" was a voyage guided by her unwavering faith in God. In this chapter, we will explore the foundational role that faith plays in the process of wise courtship. Whether you are just beginning your journey or have been on it for some time, understanding the significance of faith is paramount.

The Role of Faith in Christian Courtship

Faith is the cornerstone of Emily's journey, and it should be for anyone seeking a Christian courtship. It's the belief that God has a plan, a plan that includes your love life. The Bible reminds us in Proverbs 3:5-6, "Trust in the Lord with all your heart, and do not lean on your own understanding. In all your ways acknowledge Him, and He will make straight your paths." This verse encapsulates the essence of faith in courtship.

In her quest, Emily had to trust in the divine timing and wisdom of God. She realized that this journey might not follow the timeline or path she had in mind. It required faith to wait patiently, trusting that God's plan was perfect.

The Power of Prayer

Emily's daily life was steeped in prayer. She prayed for guidance, discernment, and strength. Prayer was her lifeline, her way of seeking God's will. Prayer, in the context of Christian courtship, is not just about asking for what you want but aligning your desires with God's plan. It's about surrendering to God and allowing Him to lead.

In 1 Thessalonians 5:17, the Bible instructs us to "pray without ceasing." This means that in every step of the courtship journey, prayer is essential. Emily sought God's guidance not only in her decision-making but also in the qualities and values she sought in a partner. She trusted that God would bring someone into her life who shared her faith and values.

Self-Discovery and Readiness

Before embarking on the journey of courtship, it's crucial to engage in self-discovery and ensure you are ready for a committed relationship. This process involves reflecting on your own values, strengths, and areas where you may need growth.

Emily spent time examining her own heart, understanding her core values, and identifying areas in her life where she could improve. Self-discovery is not just about finding the perfect partner but also becoming the best version of yourself.

In Psalm 139:23-24, the psalmist prays, "Search me, O God, and know my heart; test me and know my anxious thoughts. See if there is any offensive way in me, and lead me in the way everlasting." This prayer is a beautiful example of the self-examination and readiness that are essential before entering into a Christian courtship.

Trusting God's Timing

Emily's journey was often marked by moments of waiting. Waiting for the right person, waiting for the right time. This waiting is not a passive state but a time to grow in faith and prepare for what lies ahead.

The Bible reassures us in Ecclesiastes 3:1, "For everything there is a season, and a time for every matter under heaven." Trusting God's timing means acknowledging that He knows when you are ready and when the right person will enter your life.

In this chapter, we have delved into the foundation of faith in Christian courtship. Faith is not just a belief but an active and unwavering trust in God's plan. It involves prayer, self-discovery, and a deep understanding of God's perfect timing. As you continue your journey, keep faith as your guide, just as Emily did on her quest to find "The One." In the following chapters, we will explore practical steps and insights to help you navigate the path of wise courtship with faith as your constant companion.

3

Preparing Your Heart and Mind

Title: "Wise Courtship: A Christian Guide to Finding The One"

As Emily continued her journey in search of "The One," she realized that preparing her heart and mind was an essential step in the process of wise courtship. In this chapter, we will explore the significance of emotional and mental readiness and the steps you can take to ensure you are fully prepared for the journey of finding your life partner.

Understanding Emotional Readiness

Emotional readiness is a critical component of a successful Christian courtship. It involves being in touch with your own emotions and understanding how they can impact your relationships. The Bible encourages us in Proverbs 4:23 to "Guard your heart above all else, for it determines the course of your life."

1. Self-awareness: Emily spent time reflecting on her past relationships and experiences. This self-awareness allowed her to identify any emotional wounds, patterns, or insecurities that might hinder her future relationship.

PREPARING YOUR HEART AND MIND

Before seeking "The One," it's vital to understand and address any unresolved emotional issues.

2. Healing: Emily also understood the importance of emotional healing. This healing process may involve forgiveness, counseling, or seeking support from a trusted Christian community. Emotional healing allows you to approach courtship with a whole and healthy heart.

The Power of a Renewed Mind

In Romans 12:2, the Bible instructs us, "Do not conform to the pattern of this world, but be transformed by the renewing of your mind." Preparing your mind for Christian courtship means aligning your thoughts and beliefs with biblical principles.

1. Aligning beliefs: Emily realized the importance of aligning her beliefs about love and relationships with Christian values. This involved unlearning unhealthy beliefs and embracing God's truth about love, purity, and commitment.

2. Practicing discernment: Wise courtship requires discernment in choosing a partner. This discernment is rooted in a renewed mind that can identify character, values, and compatibility with Christian principles.

Developing a Strong Support System

Emily found strength in her Christian community, and this support system was invaluable on her journey. Ecclesiastes 4:9-10 says, "Two are better than one because they have a good return for their labor. For if either of them falls, the one will lift up his companion." Your support system can include family, friends, mentors, and fellow believers.

1. Accountability: Emily surrounded herself with people who held her

accountable for her actions and choices. Accountability is vital in maintaining purity and faithfulness in a Christian courtship.

2. Prayer partners: Having friends or mentors who join you in prayer is a powerful resource. They can provide guidance, encouragement, and a spiritual perspective on your journey.

Patience and Contentment

In Philippians 4:11-12, the apostle Paul wrote, "I have learned to be content whatever the circumstances." Contentment is a key component of emotional readiness. Emily understood that being content in her current season of singleness was crucial before seeking a partner. Patience is a virtue, and trusting God's timing is an essential aspect of emotional readiness.

Conclusion

Preparing your heart and mind for Christian courtship is a vital step on the journey to finding "The One." It involves emotional healing, aligning your beliefs with Christian principles, developing a strong support system, and cultivating patience and contentment. Emily's journey was marked by these preparations, which empowered her to approach courtship with confidence and faith.

In the following chapters, we will delve into practical steps for meeting potential partners, discerning their compatibility with your Christian values, and progressing towards a God-ordained relationship. But remember, the foundation of emotional and mental readiness is what will sustain you on this journey.

4

Navigating the Dating Landscape

Title: "Wise Courtship: A Christian Guide to Finding The One"

As Emily continued her quest to find "The One," she knew that navigating the dating landscape as a Christian required wisdom, discernment, and a commitment to her faith. In this chapter, we will explore the practical aspects of dating within the context of Christian courtship.

Christian Dating: A Different Perspective

Before Emily ventured into the world of dating, she understood the need for a distinctively Christian perspective. Christian dating is not just about finding a romantic partner but also about finding a partner who shares your faith and values. Proverbs 19:14 says, "Houses and wealth are inherited from parents, but a prudent wife is from the Lord." Emily sought a relationship that was God-ordained and not merely a product of chance or societal pressures.

1. Purity and Boundaries: Emily embraced the idea of purity in dating, both physical and emotional. She set clear boundaries to ensure that her interactions with potential partners respected her commitment to her Christian values. 1 Thessalonians 4:3-5 guided her: "For this is the will of

God, your sanctification: that you abstain from sexual immorality; that each one of you know how to control his own body in holiness and honor, not in the passion of lust."

2. Prayerful Dating: Prayer remained a cornerstone of Emily's dating experiences. She prayed before, during, and after each date, seeking God's guidance and discernment. Psalm 37:4 reminds us, "Delight yourself in the Lord, and He will give you the desires of your heart." Emily believed that delighting in the Lord included seeking His guidance in her dating decisions.

Meeting Potential Partners

Emily was intentional about where and how she met potential partners. She believed that God could guide her to the right person through various avenues.

1. Church and Christian Events: Emily actively participated in church events, Bible studies, and Christian gatherings. These were places where she could meet like-minded individuals who shared her faith.

2. Online Dating: In today's digital age, Emily realized that online dating could be a useful tool if used wisely. She chose reputable Christian dating platforms and was clear about her values and expectations in her online profile.

3. Friendships: Emily also recognized the potential of her existing friendships. Sometimes, a close friend could become a romantic partner if there was mutual interest and shared values.

Discerning Compatibility

When dating, it's essential to assess compatibility not just in terms of interests and hobbies but also in terms of core values and faith. Amos 3:3 asks, "Do two walk together unless they have agreed to do so?" Emily understood the importance of walking together in faith and values with her potential partner.

1. Deep Conversations: Emily engaged in meaningful conversations with her dates. These conversations helped her assess whether their faith, values, and life goals aligned.

2. Observing Character: Emily paid close attention to the character of her potential partners. She looked for qualities like integrity, kindness, and a commitment to their Christian faith.

The Role of Family and Community

Family and community support were invaluable to Emily. She involved her trusted loved ones in her dating journey and valued their input. Proverbs 15:22 says, "Without counsel, plans fail, but with many advisers, they succeed."

Conclusion

Navigating the dating landscape as a Christian requires a unique perspective that aligns with your faith and values. Emily's journey was marked by purity, prayer, intentionality, and discernment in her dating experiences. Remember that while the practical aspects of dating are important, they should always be guided by your commitment to your Christian faith.

In the following chapters, we will delve into the development of a deeper connection with a potential partner, the importance of communication, and the process of discerning whether this person might be "The One" whom God has chosen for you. Stay true to your faith and values as you journey through the world of Christian courtship.

5

Building a Deeper Connection

Title: "Wise Courtship: A Christian Guide to Finding The One"

Emily's journey to find "The One" had led her through the foundational stages of faith, emotional readiness, and the world of Christian dating. Now, she found herself at a crucial juncture – building a deeper connection with someone she had met on her journey. In this chapter, we will explore how to foster a deeper connection while staying true to Christian principles.

The Importance of Genuine Communication

Proverbs 16:24 tells us, "Gracious words are like a honeycomb, sweetness to the soul and health to the body." Genuine and open communication forms the bedrock of a strong and meaningful connection. Emily knew that building a deeper relationship required the exchange of thoughts, feelings, and experiences.

1. Active Listening: Emily practiced active listening during her conversations. She focused on what her partner was saying rather than thinking about her response. Active listening creates an atmosphere of trust and understanding.

2. Vulnerability: Sharing one's thoughts and emotions can be intimidating, but it's essential for building a deeper connection. Emily and her partner opened up to each other about their dreams, fears, and experiences.

3. Honesty: Honesty is a fundamental Christian value. Emily and her partner were honest about their beliefs, values, and past experiences. This ensured that there were no hidden agendas or misunderstandings.

Cultivating Shared Experiences

A strong connection is often built on shared experiences. Emily and her partner sought opportunities to create memories together.

1. Spiritual Experiences: They attended church services, participated in prayer meetings, and engaged in spiritual growth activities together. This allowed them to grow in their faith as a couple.

2. Service and Outreach: Emily and her partner found common ground in their desire to serve others. Volunteering together created a deeper bond as they worked toward a shared goal of helping those in need.

3. Leisure and Hobbies: Finding common hobbies and interests can be fun and rewarding. Emily and her partner enjoyed hiking, reading, and cooking together, which created moments of joy and connection.

Navigating Challenges Together

No relationship is without its challenges. Emily and her partner encountered difficulties along the way, and they approached them as opportunities to grow closer.

1. Conflict Resolution: They used Christian principles of forgiveness and reconciliation to navigate conflicts. Matthew 18:15 guides us: "If your brother

or sister sins, go and point out their fault, just between the two of you."

2. Prayer in Times of Trouble: Emily and her partner turned to prayer when facing challenges. This brought them closer to God and to each other.

Seeking God's Guidance

Throughout the journey of building a deeper connection, Emily and her partner continued to seek God's guidance. Proverbs 3:6 was their anchor: "In all your ways acknowledge Him, and He will make your paths straight."

1. Prayer as a Couple: They prayed together, seeking God's wisdom in their relationship. This not only deepened their connection but also strengthened their faith.

2. Counsel from Wise Mentors: Emily and her partner also sought counsel from trusted mentors and spiritual leaders who could provide guidance and insight.

Conclusion

Building a deeper connection in Christian courtship is a journey that involves genuine communication, shared experiences, and navigating challenges together. At the heart of it all is the commitment to seek God's guidance and to keep your faith and values at the center of your relationship.

In the following chapters, we will explore the discernment process of whether the person you are building this connection with is "The One" whom God has chosen for you. Emily's journey serves as a testament to the power of faith, love, and wisdom in Christian courtship.

6

Discerning "The One"

Title: "Wise Courtship: A Christian Guide to Finding The One"

As Emily's relationship deepened, she faced a pivotal moment in her journey – the process of discerning whether the person she was building a connection with was indeed "The One" whom God had chosen for her. In this chapter, we will explore the art of discernment in Christian courtship.

Seeking God's Will

Proverbs 3:5-6 reminds us, "Trust in the Lord with all your heart and lean not on your understanding; in all your ways submit to Him, and He will make your paths straight." Discernment in Christian courtship begins with a deep trust in God's wisdom and timing.

1. Prayerful Discernment: Emily and her partner continued to seek God's guidance through prayer. They prayed individually and as a couple, asking for clarity and peace regarding their future together.

2. Listening to God's Voice: They listened for God's guidance in their hearts and through scripture. Sometimes, a specific Bible verse or a feeling of peace served as a confirmation of their path.

Evaluating Compatibility

Discernment involves evaluating the compatibility of values, goals, and the potential for a lifelong partnership.

1. Shared Values: Emily and her partner continued to discuss their core values, ensuring that their beliefs aligned. They understood that shared faith and values were the foundation of a lasting relationship.

2. Life Goals: They talked about their aspirations and life goals, ensuring they complemented each other's dreams. They shared a common vision for their future.

Seeking Wise Counsel

Proverbs 15:22 advises, "Plans fail for lack of counsel, but with many advisers, they succeed." Emily and her partner sought counsel from trusted mentors, family members, and spiritual leaders.

1. Trusted Mentors: They shared their thoughts and feelings with mentors who provided invaluable insights and guidance. These mentors had experience in Christian courtship and marriage.

2. Family Input: Emily and her partner sought input from their families, who knew them well and could offer a broader perspective.

Embracing Peace and Confirmation

Colossians 3:15 says, "Let the peace of Christ rule in your hearts." Peace and confirmation are powerful indicators of God's will in discernment.

1. Inner Peace: Emily and her partner paid close attention to the peace they felt in their hearts. They knew that a sense of inner calm and confidence was a sign of God's confirmation.

2. Mutual Agreement: They reached a mutual agreement that they were both ready for a lifelong commitment. This consensus was a confirmation of their path.

Conclusion

Discernment is a deeply spiritual and prayerful process. It's about seeking God's will, evaluating compatibility, seeking wise counsel, and embracing peace and confirmation. Emily and her partner found that discernment brought them closer to God's plan for their lives and their relationship.

In the next and final chapter, we will explore the beautiful journey of commitment and the steps Emily took to seal her love with the person she believed God had chosen for her. The story of Emily's wise courtship is a testament to the power of faith, patience, and discernment in finding "The One."

7

The Journey of Commitment

Title: "Wise Courtship: A Christian Guide to Finding The One"

Emily's journey had been a testament to faith, wisdom, and the power of prayer. In this final chapter, we'll explore the beautiful journey of commitment, as Emily sealed her love with the person she believed God had chosen for her.

The Covenant of Commitment

As they moved toward deeper commitment, Emily and her partner recognized that their love was not just a feeling but a choice and a covenant. In Christian courtship, commitment is a sacred promise to one another and to God.

1. Preparation for Commitment: Before making a formal commitment, Emily and her partner spent time in prayer and self-reflection. They sought to ensure they were fully ready to enter into this covenant.

2. Ceremony of Commitment: They chose to mark their commitment with a special ceremony attended by family and close friends. In this ceremony,

they made vows to each other and before God.

The Role of Christian Marriage Counseling

Before they formalized their commitment, Emily and her partner engaged in Christian marriage counseling. This counseling served as a foundation for their future together.

1. Counseling Process: They met with a Christian marriage counselor who provided guidance on various aspects of marriage, including communication, conflict resolution, and maintaining a strong spiritual connection.

2. Preparation for Challenges: They recognized that marriage would come with its share of challenges and obstacles. Counseling prepared them to face these challenges with faith and resilience.

Keeping God at the Center

Proverbs 3:6 advises, "In all your ways acknowledge Him, and He will make your paths straight." As they made their commitment, Emily and her partner made a firm commitment to keep God at the center of their relationship.

1. Spiritual Practices: They continued their spiritual practices together, attending church services, engaging in prayer, and studying the Bible. This maintained the spiritual bond they had built.

2. Praying Together: They committed to regular prayer as a couple, seeking God's guidance and strength for their journey.

Building a Strong Foundation

Their journey of commitment was about building a strong foundation for their future together. They recognized that their commitment was not just for the present but for the rest of their lives.

1. Shared Vision: They continued to discuss their shared vision for the future. They set goals, both individual and as a couple, to work toward.

2. Serving Together: Emily and her partner actively sought opportunities to serve others together, recognizing that a life of service was a key component of their commitment.

The Blessings of Christian Commitment

As they formalized their commitment, Emily and her partner experienced the blessings of God's design for love and marriage. Proverbs 18:22 reminds us, "He who finds a wife finds what is good and receives favor from the Lord."

1. A Lifelong Partnership: They embraced the idea of a lifelong partnership, trusting that God had brought them together for a purpose.

2. The Journey Continues: Their journey was far from over; it was just the beginning of a lifetime of love, faith, and growth together.

Conclusion

The journey of commitment in Christian courtship is a beautiful testament to the power of faith and love. Emily and her partner understood that their commitment was a sacred covenant with God, and it was rooted in shared values, a strong foundation, and a commitment to keeping God at the center of their relationship.

As we conclude this guide, remember that finding "The One" in Christian courtship is not just about the destination but also the journey itself. May you find inspiration in Emily's story and the principles of faith, wisdom, discernment, and commitment as you embark on your own quest to find

"The One" whom God has chosen for you.

8

A Lifelong Journey

Title: "Wise Courtship: A Christian Guide to Finding The One"

In this final chapter, we step back from Emily's journey and explore the lifelong aspects of wise courtship as a Christian. Finding "The One" is not just about the courtship phase; it's a journey that continues through marriage and beyond.

The Journey of Marriage

Marriage is the culmination of the courtship journey. It's a commitment to love, honor, and cherish each other in God's name. But it's also the beginning of a new chapter in your journey.

1. Ephesians 5:25-26: These verses remind us of the depth of love and sacrifice required in marriage. "Husbands, love your wives, just as Christ loved the church and gave himself up for her to make her holy."

2. Continued Growth: Marriage is an opportunity for continued growth as a couple. Emily and her partner recognized that they would face challenges

and joys together, and their commitment to each other and to God would be their guide.

The Role of Faith

Throughout the lifelong journey of Christian courtship, faith remains at the heart of the relationship. It's not just a part of the courtship phase but a vital thread that runs through the entire journey.

1. Proverbs 3:5-6: These verses, mentioned earlier, continue to guide Emily and her partner as they navigate the highs and lows of married life. Trust in the Lord and acknowledge Him in all aspects of your life.

2. Spiritual Bond: A strong spiritual bond is crucial in marriage. It's nurtured through shared spiritual practices, prayer, and active participation in a Christian community.

Renewed Commitment

Marriage requires a commitment that is not static but constantly renewed. Emily and her partner understood the importance of renewing their commitment to each other and to God.

1. Renewing Vows: Periodic vow renewals served as a reminder of their initial commitment and their continued love for each other.

2. Rekindling the Flame: Marriage is a lifelong journey of rekindling the flame of love and passion. This rekindling is an essential part of a healthy and thriving relationship.

Challenges and Triumphs

Emily's journey was marked by both challenges and triumphs. She knew that marriage, like courtship, would have its share of difficulties. It was their shared commitment and faith that helped them navigate these challenges.

1. 1 Peter 4:8: "Above all, love each other deeply because love covers over a multitude of sins." Emily and her partner understood the power of love and forgiveness in overcoming challenges.

2. Shared Support System: Just as in courtship, their support system of family, mentors, and friends continued to play a crucial role in their married life.

Conclusion

The journey of wise courtship as a Christian is not a finite one; it's a lifelong journey of love, faith, and commitment. As we conclude this guide, may you carry with you the principles of faith, wisdom, discernment, and commitment into your own journey to find "The One." Emily's story is a testament to the beauty of a Christian courtship and the enduring love that results from following God's guidance in the quest for true and lasting love.

Remember that your journey is unique, and God has a plan for your love life. May you find inspiration, guidance, and strength in your own journey as you seek to find "The One" whom God has chosen for you.

9

Nurturing Love and Partnership

Title: "Wise Courtship: A Christian Guide to Finding The One"

In this chapter, we'll delve into the ongoing journey of nurturing love and partnership once you've found "The One." While courtship and marriage are significant milestones, they mark the beginning of a lifelong adventure together. Emily's story reminds us that a Christian relationship doesn't end at the altar; it's a continuous journey of growth, love, and devotion.

The Journey Beyond Marriage

Emily's courtship journey led her to a profound commitment, and her wedding day was a joyous celebration of love. However, she understood that marriage was just the starting point. As Proverbs 5:18 reminds us, "Let your fountain be blessed, and rejoice in the wife of your youth."

1. Ephesians 5:21: Marriage is a partnership, and the verse, "Submit to one another out of reverence for Christ," was a guiding principle for Emily and her partner. They understood that mutual respect and submission were keys

to a harmonious relationship.

2. Continual Growth: Love in a Christian marriage is not static; it's an ever-evolving journey. Emily's partner and she recognized that their relationship required ongoing growth, nurturing, and attention.

Maintaining a Strong Spiritual Connection

Emily's faith had been central to her courtship journey, and she knew that it must continue to be at the heart of her marriage. The spiritual connection that they had built throughout courtship needed to be nurtured in marriage.

1. Shared Devotions: Emily and her partner continued their practice of shared devotions, Bible study, and prayer. This not only strengthened their spiritual bond but also brought them closer to God as a couple.

2. Church and Community: Actively participating in their Christian community remained a vital aspect of their marriage. They saw their involvement in church and community service as a way of not only giving back but also deepening their bond as a couple.

Effective Communication

Proverbs 18:21 states, "The tongue has the power of life and death." Emily's partner and she understood the significance of effective communication in maintaining a healthy marriage.

1. Listening and Empathy: They continued to practice active listening and empathy in their conversations. They made an effort to understand each other's thoughts and feelings, fostering a deeper connection.

2. Conflict Resolution: They approached conflicts with a mindset of resolution and forgiveness. Matthew 18:15 guided their approach: "If your

brother or sister sins, go and point out their fault, just between the two of you."

Nurturing Love and Romance

Love and romance are not finite resources; they can be nurtured and expanded over time. Emily knew that keeping the flame of love alive required effort and creativity.

1. Date Nights: Regular date nights were a way to keep the romance alive. These nights provided an opportunity to rekindle the spark and enjoy quality time together.

2. Surprises and Gestures: Surprising each other with small acts of love and appreciation was a part of their routine. These gestures kept the relationship fresh and exciting.

A Lifelong Journey

Emily's journey serves as a reminder that a Christian courtship is not a destination but a lifelong journey. As 1 Corinthians 13:4-7 beautifully articulates, "Love is patient, love is kind. It does not envy, it does not boast, it is not proud."

1. Growing Together: Emily and her partner were committed to growing together in love, faith, and partnership. They knew that their journey was a testament to God's grace and guidance.

2. A Testimony of Faith: Their relationship was a testimony of faith in action, reflecting the love and wisdom of God.

Conclusion

As you continue your own journey of Christian courtship and marriage, may you find inspiration in the ongoing story of Emily and her partner. Remember that love and partnership require effort, faith, and commitment. This journey is a testament to the power of faith, love, and wisdom in the quest for a lasting and meaningful relationship. May your journey be a testament to God's grace and guidance, and may you continue to nurture love and partnership throughout your lives.

10

Weathering Life's Storms

Title: "Wise Courtship: A Christian Guide to Finding The One"

As Emily and her partner embarked on their journey of commitment and marriage, they knew that life was filled with ups and downs. In this chapter, we will explore how a Christian relationship can weather life's storms and emerge stronger on the other side.

The Inevitability of Challenges

Challenges are an unavoidable part of life. Emily understood that her relationship would face its share of difficulties, and they were committed to navigating these challenges with faith and resilience.

1. 1 Peter 4:12-13: The Bible reminds us that trials are a part of life, but they also present opportunities for growth. "Dear friends, do not be surprised at the fiery ordeal that has come on you to test you. But rejoice inasmuch as you participate in the sufferings of Christ, so that you may be overjoyed when his glory is revealed."

2. Shared Support System: Emily and her partner knew that relying on their trusted support system of family, mentors, and friends would be crucial during challenging times.

Unity in Adversity

Adversity can either draw a couple closer or push them apart. Emily and her partner were determined to allow challenges to strengthen their bond.

1. Ephesians 4:2-3: "Be completely humble and gentle; be patient, bearing with one another in love. Make every effort to keep the unity of the Spirit through the bond of peace." These verses guided their approach to challenges, emphasizing patience and unity.

2. Communication: Open and honest communication was key to addressing issues and conflicts. Emily and her partner practiced active listening and empathy to understand each other's perspectives.

The Role of Faith

Their faith remained central in their approach to adversity. They saw trials as opportunities to lean on God and trust in His plan.

1. James 1:2-4: "Consider it pure joy, my brothers and sisters, whenever you face trials of many kinds, because you know that the testing of your faith produces perseverance." Emily and her partner viewed challenges as opportunities to strengthen their faith and perseverance.

2. Prayer: They continued to pray individually and as a couple, seeking God's guidance and strength in facing life's storms. Prayer was their source of comfort and wisdom.

Support and Counseling

There were times when Emily and her partner sought counseling from Christian professionals to help them navigate challenges. They understood that seeking help was a sign of strength, not weakness.

1. Proverbs 11:14: "For lack of guidance a nation falls, but victory is won through many advisers." They applied this principle to their relationship, seeking guidance from wise counselors.

2. Marriage Enrichment: Periodic marriage enrichment programs and retreats served as opportunities to strengthen their bond and learn valuable tools for facing life's storms.

Growing Stronger Together

While the storms of life are inevitable, Emily and her partner believed that they could emerge from each challenge stronger and more deeply connected.

1. Romans 5:3-4: "Not only so, but we also glory in our sufferings because we know that suffering produces perseverance; perseverance, character; and character, hope." They approached adversity with a mindset of perseverance and the hope of a stronger, deeper love.

2. Rekindling Love: After each storm, they made a conscious effort to rekindle the flame of love and remind each other of their commitment.

Conclusion

Life's storms are a reality, but with faith, unity, and a commitment to supporting one another, a Christian relationship can weather even the fiercest challenges. Emily's journey serves as a testament to the power of faith, love, and wisdom in navigating the trials of life. As you continue your own journey in finding and nurturing "The One," may you find inspiration in the principles of faith, resilience, and unity. Remember, it's not about avoiding storms but about learning to dance in the rain together.

11

Chapter 11

Chapter 11: A Legacy of Love

Title: "Wise Courtship: A Christian Guide to Finding The One"

In this chapter, we will explore the concept of leaving a legacy of love within a Christian relationship. Emily's journey to find "The One" didn't just end with her courtship and marriage; it was a lifelong commitment to building a legacy of love that would impact future generations.

The Enduring Legacy

As Emily and her partner continued their journey through life, they recognized that their love was not only meant for themselves but to be shared and passed down as a legacy to their children and future generations.

1. Deuteronomy 6:6-7: "These commandments that I give you today are to be on your hearts. Impress them on your children. Talk about them when you sit at home and when you walk along the road when you lie down and when you get up." This verse exemplifies the importance of passing down God's love and wisdom.

2. Legacy of Faith: Emily and her partner's commitment to faith and love would be their most significant legacy. They aimed to instill Christian values and the importance of love, forgiveness, and respect in their children.

Intergenerational Blessings

A Christian legacy of love is not only about teaching but also about setting an example through actions and attitudes. Emily and her partner were determined to create a legacy that would bless their children and grandchildren.

1. Proverbs 13:22: "A good person leaves an inheritance for their children's children, but a sinner's wealth is stored up for the righteous." Emily and her partner aimed to leave a spiritual and emotional inheritance for their descendants.

2. Modeling Love: They knew that the best way to teach love was to demonstrate it. They strived to treat each other with love and respect, providing a living example of a godly marriage.

Family Traditions

Emily and her partner established family traditions rooted in their Christian faith. These traditions were designed to create lasting memories and deepen their family's spiritual connection.

1. Celebrating Faith: They celebrated religious holidays and traditions that were meaningful to their faith, making sure to pass down the significance to their children.

2. Family Devotions: Regular family devotions, Bible readings, and prayer times were established to nurture their children's spiritual growth.

Parenting with Love

CHAPTER 11

Emily and her partner understood that their role as parents was crucial in building a legacy of love. They aimed to be intentional in their parenting approach, emphasizing love, discipline, and faith.

1. Ephesians 6:4: "Fathers, do not exasperate your children; instead, bring them up in the training and instruction of the Lord." This verse guided their parenting philosophy, emphasizing love, discipline, and faith as integral components.

2. Teaching Values: They actively taught their children Christian values, such as kindness, forgiveness, and service to others. Their goal was to raise children who understood the importance of love in all its forms.

Supporting Future Relationships

A legacy of love extends beyond the immediate family. Emily and her partner aimed to equip their children to make wise choices in their own relationships.

1. Proverbs 22:6: "Start children off on the way they should go, and even when they are old, they will not turn from it." They understood the importance of providing a foundation for their children to build healthy, loving relationships in the future.

2. Counsel and Guidance: They committed to being a source of counsel and guidance for their children as they navigated their own paths to finding "The One."

Conclusion

A legacy of love within a Christian relationship is a beautiful way to ensure that the values of faith, love, and wisdom are passed down through generations. Emily's journey serves as a testament to the power of love and faith in building a legacy that leaves a lasting impact on those who come after us.

As you continue your own journey to find and nurture "The One," consider the legacy of love you want to leave behind. May you find inspiration in the principles of faith, intentionality, and love as you strive to build a legacy that blesses future generations with the enduring love of God.

12

Celebrating a Lifetime of Love

Title: "Wise Courtship: A Christian Guide to Finding The One"

In this final chapter, we will explore the importance of celebrating a lifetime of love in a Christian relationship. Emily's journey to find "The One" had been a testament to the power of faith, wisdom, and love. As she and her partner continued to build their life together, they embraced the concept of celebrating their enduring love.

The Significance of Celebration

A Christian relationship is not just about finding "The One" but also about cherishing and celebrating that love throughout a lifetime. Celebrations mark important milestones, reaffirm commitments, and create lasting memories.

1. Genesis 2:24: "Therefore a man shall leave his father and his mother and hold fast to his wife, and they shall become one flesh." Celebrating your union is a way of holding fast to the commitment you made to one another.

2. Anniversaries: Emily and her partner marked each year of their marriage with a special anniversary celebration. It was a time to reflect on their journey

and reaffirm their love and commitment.

Renewing Vows

As the years passed, Emily and her partner chose to renew their vows in a meaningful ceremony surrounded by family and friends. This act served as a powerful way to recommit to their love and their faith.

1. Ecclesiastes 4:12: "Though one may be overpowered, two can defend themselves. A cord of three strands is not quickly broken." In their vow renewal ceremony, they included a third strand in their cord, symbolizing the presence of God in their union.

2. Rekindling Love: Renewing vows was not just a ceremony but an opportunity to rekindle their love and deepen their connection. It allowed them to reflect on their journey together and the blessings they had received.

Passing Down Wisdom

Emily and her partner saw their journey as an opportunity to pass down wisdom and experiences to their children and grandchildren. They understood that the lessons they had learned could benefit future generations.

1. Proverbs 4:6-7: "Do not forsake wisdom, and she will protect you; love her, and she will watch over you. The beginning of wisdom is this: Get wisdom. Though it cost all you have, get understanding." They aimed to share the wisdom they had gained on their journey.

2. Storytelling: They shared their own love story and the lessons they had learned with their children and grandchildren. It served as a valuable source of guidance for the younger generations.

Celebrating Milestones

Life is marked by various milestones, and Emily and her partner celebrated these moments as a way of appreciating the journey they had taken together.

1. Proverbs 16:9: "In their hearts, humans plan their course, but the Lord establishes their steps." They saw milestones as reflections of God's plan for their lives.

2. Family Gatherings: Milestones like graduations, weddings, and the birth of grandchildren were celebrated with family gatherings, reinforcing the importance of faith and love within their family.

Giving Back

As their love story continued, Emily and her partner saw the importance of giving back to their community and church. They believed that their love and blessings were meant to be shared.

1. Matthew 5:16: "In the same way, let your light shine before others, that they may see your good deeds and glorify your Father in heaven." They sought to shine their light by giving back through acts of service and kindness.

2. Mentoring and Guidance: They provided guidance and mentoring to younger couples and individuals who were on their own journeys to find "The One."

Conclusion

Emily's journey was a testament to the power of faith, wisdom, and love in finding and nurturing "The One." The final chapter of celebrating a lifetime of love serves as a reminder that a Christian relationship is not just a moment but a lifelong journey filled with love, faith, and wisdom. May your own journey be marked by celebrations of love, wisdom passed down, and a commitment to giving back, all underpinned by the enduring love of God.

WISE COURTSHIP: A CHRISTIAN GUIDE TO FINDING THE ONE

Book Summary: "Wise Courtship: A Christian Guide to Finding The One"

In "Wise Courtship: A Christian Guide to Finding The One," we follow the inspirational journey of Emily as she navigates the often complex and challenging path to finding "The One" in the context of her Christian faith. This guide is not just a story; it's a comprehensive resource that combines storytelling with valuable insights and guidance for those seeking a meaningful and God-centered relationship.

The book is divided into twelve chapters, each exploring a unique aspect of wise courtship in a Christian context:

Chapter 1: Preparing Your Heart
Emily's journey begins with the foundational step of preparing her heart for a relationship. This chapter emphasizes the importance of faith, self-awareness, and emotional readiness.

Chapter 2: Navigating Christian Dating
Emily delves into the world of Christian dating, discussing principles, values, and the search for compatibility while staying true to her faith.

Chapter 3: The Power of Prayer
Prayer becomes a central theme in Emily's journey as she realizes the significance of seeking God's guidance in her quest to find "The One."

Chapter 4: Building Meaningful Connections
The fourth chapter explores the process of building meaningful connections with potential partners, focusing on shared values and the development of a strong emotional bond.

Chapter 5: Building a Deeper Connection
In this chapter, Emily goes beyond the surface and delves into fostering a deeper connection, emphasizing honest communication, shared experiences,

and spiritual growth.

Chapter 6: Discerning "The One"
Emily reaches a critical juncture where she must discern whether the person she's building a connection with is truly "The One" chosen by God.

Chapter 7: The Journey of Commitment
As the relationship deepens, Emily and her partner formalize their commitment through a ceremony and prepare for a lifelong journey together.

Chapter 8: A Lifelong Journey
Emily's journey continues into the realm of marriage, emphasizing the importance of faith, maintaining a strong spiritual connection, and keeping God at the center of their relationship.

Chapter 9: Weathering Life's Storms
Life's challenges are explored in this chapter, highlighting the importance of unity, effective communication, and the role of faith in overcoming difficulties.

Chapter 10: Nurturing Love and Partnership
This chapter discusses how to nurture and strengthen love and partnership, emphasizing date nights, gestures of love, and ongoing growth as a couple.

Chapter 11: A Legacy of Love
Emily and her partner recognize the importance of creating a legacy of love for their children and future generations, passing down wisdom and values.

Chapter 12: Celebrating a Lifetime of Love
In the final chapter, Emily celebrates the enduring love that she and her partner have built throughout their journey, marked by renewing vows, passing down wisdom, celebrating milestones, and giving back to the community.

Throughout the book, "Wise Courtship: A Christian Guide to Finding The One" combines biblical wisdom with real-life experiences to provide a comprehensive guide for individuals seeking a Christian-centered approach to courtship and lasting love. Emily's journey is a testament to the power of faith, wisdom, and love in finding and nurturing "The One" chosen by God.

www.ingramcontent.com/pod-product-compliance
Lightning Source LLC
LaVergne TN
LVHW010438070526
838199LV00066B/6072